FIND OUT ABOUT

Pushes and Pulls

Terry Jennings

BBC

© **Terry Jennings/BBC Education**

BBC Education
201 Wood Lane
London W12 7TS

ISBN 0 563 37467 5

Editor: Caroline White
Designer: Clare Davey
Picture researcher: Emma Segal
Educational advisers: Samina Miller, Shelagh Scarborough
Photographer: Simon Pugh

With grateful thanks to:
Elizabeth Cranney, Adam King, Meera Patel, Daniel Salvador, Jemma Samuel

Researched photographs © Allsport (page 16 bottom); Ecoscene (pages 5 right, and 20 bottom); Ford Motor Company (page 9); Robert Harding Picture Library (page 20 top), Images Colour Library (page 22); Science Photo Library (pages 5 left, 10 bottom, and 17); SuperStock (page 16 right)

Printed in Belgium by Proost
reprinted 2000

Contents

You move a bicycle by **pushing** and **pulling**.

You **push** a frisbee through the air when you throw it.

How do we move things?

Things do not move by themselves. Everything needs a push or a pull to make it move. These pushes and pulls are called forces. You have to push down on the pedals of a bicycle to make the wheels go round. The bicycle will change direction if you pull on the handlebars. It will stop if you pull on the brakes.

Some pushes and pulls are small. Others are very big. Cars, lorries and trains do not move unless they are given a big push or pull by their engines.

This bulldozer makes a big **push**.

This lorry can **pull** very hard.

Which way will the sledge move when the girl **pushes** it?

Which way will the sledge move when the girl **pulls** it?

How is it different if the girl pulls the sledge with **two** children on it?

What do you think will happen if there are **three** children on the sledge?

Which way will it go?

Things usually move in the direction that you push or pull them. When you push something, it moves away from you. When you pull something, it moves towards you.

The bigger the object, the bigger the push or pull you need to move it. The girl can pull the sledge along easily when one person sits on it. She has to pull much harder when there are two people. If three people sit on the sledge, she may not be able to move it at all.

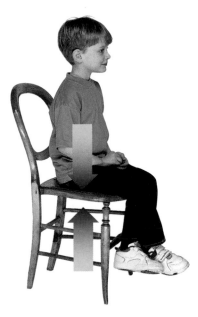

The boy's body **pushes** down on the chair. The chair holds him up and stops him falling.

You can change the shape of a balloon **pushing** air into it.

You can **push** and **pull** on plasticine to change its shape.

How can we change the shape of things?

Pushes and pulls can change the shape of things. You can change the shape of a rubber band by pulling on each end. When you blow up a balloon, you push air into it. The balloon changes shape because of the force of the air.

Things do not go on changing shape for ever. A rubber band will break if you pull on it too hard. A tree bends when a strong wind pushes against it. If the force of the wind is too great, the tree will break.

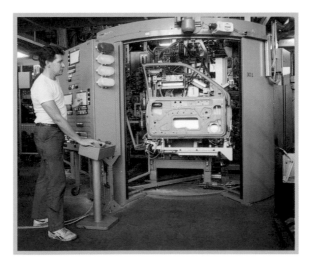

This machine **pushes** and **pulls** pieces of metal into the shape of a car door.

Why does the boy keep his **feet** up when he comes down the slide?

These tyres have thick **treads**. They help the machine to grip the ground even when it is muddy.

treads

Why do moving things stop?

Boots often have thick treads on the soles. The treads grip the ground and stop you falling over when it is icy. This is because there is lots of friction. Friction is the force that stops things sliding past each other easily.

A sledge slides easily over snow because it is smooth and there is little friction. It will not slide easily over rough grass because there is lots of friction.

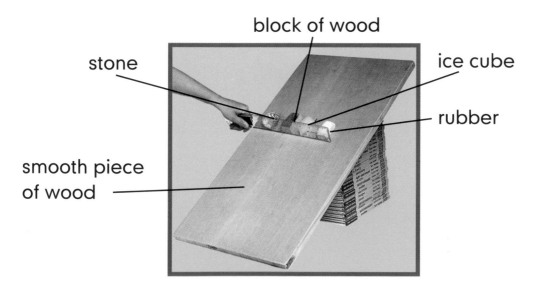

stone — block of wood — ice cube

smooth piece of wood — rubber

Find small objects made of different materials and have a race. The first object to reach the bottom of the slope has least **friction**.

Is it easier to **slide** or **roll** the tin?

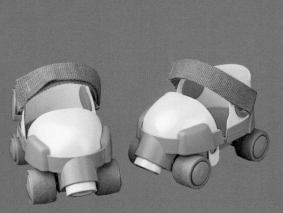

There are many different kinds of **wheels**.

How do wheels help things to move?

It is difficult to push a big box along the floor. There is too much friction when all of the box touches the ground.

You can use rollers to help move the box. Because only a small part of each roller touches the ground, there is little friction. But it is still quite hard work. You have to keep taking the rollers away from the back of the box and putting them in front. Wheels make it much easier to move or turn things.

Rollers help to move the box.

A magnet attracts things made of **iron** or **steel**.

The needle of a **compass** is a small magnet.

Magnets keep a **fridge door** closed.

Can a magnet push and pull?

Magnets have an invisible force. A magnet pulls things made of iron or steel towards it. We say the magnet attracts these metals.

Every magnet has two ends called the north pole and the south pole. If you put two north poles or two south poles together, you can feel the magnets pushing each other apart. This push is a force. The force between magnets is called a magnetic force.

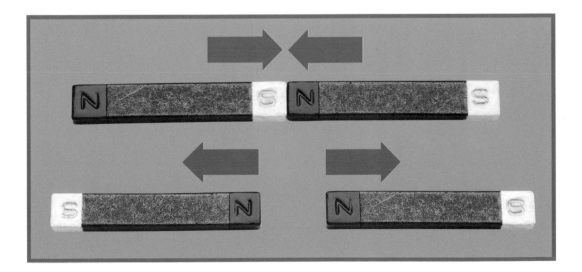

Magnets can **push** and **pull**.

Gravity makes everything fall down.

Why do things fall down?

Apples fall from trees. When you throw a ball in the air, it falls back down again. If you throw the ball higher, it still falls to the ground. Things fall down because the Earth pulls everything towards its centre. This invisible force is called gravity.

Gravity is the reason why things fall down and not up. There is little gravity in space. Things in a spaceship just float around.

Astronauts have to tie themselves down if they do not want to float about in **space**.

Which things will **float**? Which things will **sink**?

Why do some things sink?

Collect objects of the same size and put them in a bowl of water. Which float on top of the water? Which sink to the bottom? Are they heavy or light? Why do some objects float just under the water?

Roll plasticine into a ball and watch it sink. Dry the plasticine and make it into the shape of a boat. The water now has a much wider shape to push up. The boat floats because the plasticine takes up more room.

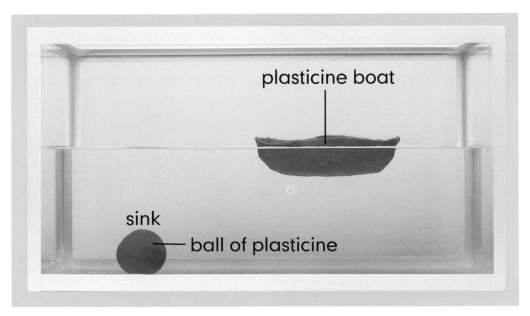

plasticine boat

sink

ball of plasticine

Why does the plasticine ball **sink**?

Air helps to keep things afloat.

Why does a steel ship **float**?

Why do some things float?

Things with air inside them float well because air is lighter than water. A ball with air inside it will float in water. If you push down on the ball, the water seems to push back. The water rises up the bucket as the ball pushes it aside.

The shape of an object is very important. A small block of steel sinks because it is heavy for its size. A huge steel ship floats. It has lots of air inside and is light for its size.

What happens if you let go of the **ball**?

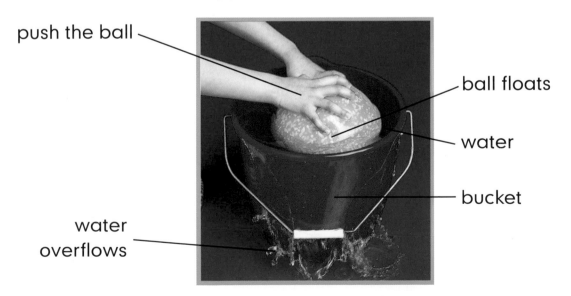

push the ball

ball floats

water

bucket

water
overflows

Why is it difficult to stop some moving things?

Once something is moving, it will keep going until a force stops it. Heavy things are difficult to stop. It can take several kilometres for a ship to stop moving. Fast things are more difficult to stop than slow things.

Bicycles and motor vehicles have brakes to stop them. Lorries are heavy and need large powerful brakes. Trains are heavier and faster than lorries. They have lots of large brakes to stop them moving.

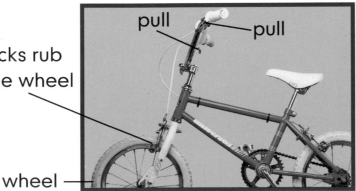

pull   pull

brake blocks rub against the wheel

wheel

A bicycle is **light** and fairly easy to stop.
It needs only **small** brakes.

Index

PRINTED IN BELGIUM BY
proost
INTERNATIONAL BOOK PRODUCTION